Angels Everywhere

by

Marcia C. Fleischman

AuthorHouse™
1663 Liberty Drive
Bloomington, IN 47403
www.authorhouse.com
Phone: 833-262-8899

Because of the dynamic nature of the Internet, any web addresses or links contained in this book may have changed
since publication and may no longer be valid. The views expressed in this work are solely those of the author and do not
necessarily reflect the views of the publisher, and the publisher hereby disclaims any responsibility for them.

Any people depicted in stock imagery provided by Getty Images are models,
and such images are being used for illustrative purposes only.
Certain stock imagery © Getty Images.

This book is printed on acid-free paper.

ISBN: 978-1-4389-2531-8 (sc)

Print information available on the last page.

Published by AuthorHouse 06/27/2023

authorHOUSE®

Angels Everywhere

by
Marcia C. Fleischman

Angels like to live everywhere.

They live on the ground.

They live in the air.

They live in the dark of night.

But they mostly like to live in the light.

Their favorite thing to do is hang out with you.

Some angels are big and tall,
and sometimes they are very small.

They hang out with their favorite people;

not just in a building with a steeple.

Angels are full of light, kindness, and love.

They are a gift from God above.

They always bring you lots of love!

They watch over you when you sleep.

Their love for you is very deep.

Very close to you they keep!

On the way to school,
they ride on your backpack,

or they ride with you in the car. That's a fact.

They sometimes have usual names,
like Sarah, Sue, John, and James.

And sometimes their names are kind of funny,
like Peace-Give-I or Near-to-the-Heart-of-God,
Lucia, Ingrid, Borat, or Jean-Claude.

They are always close when you need them;
when you're eating, playing,
or brushing your teeth.

Knowing they are there is such a relief!

There are angels that help you with all you do,
like playing soccer

or going to the zoo.

There are angels that help you play football

and angels that like to go with you to the mall.

The thing that angels do the best is love you,
and they never rest!

Angels fill you with light and lots of joy,
no matter if you are a girl or a boy.

With angels there is nothing you have to do;
just play and have fun and be the best you!

The Beginning

Printed in the United States
by Baker & Taylor Publisher Services